IMPEACHMENT AND THE MULLER EFFECT

To what extent did this report lead to the impeachment?
When a thorough analysis is done, will this be the one thing which led to the impeachment?
Although most experts may have differing opinions about who really did what and when,
in the final analysis, the Muller Effect cannot be discounted. An analysis now follows.
You be the judge. This analysis is a little over an hour but is a quick read.

07:56
There is a strike consulting work
07:59
political consulting work cost Anakin
08:01
eliminate contacts with power mana first
08:04
time with the **Trump campaign Paul**
08:06
Manafort joins the campaign for
08:07
manifests campaign period context for
08:09
mana first to campaign period were
08:12
meeting with Kostas still a chemical
08:14
emanation United States post resignation
08:17
activities post election a transition
08:19
period contacts immediate post-election
08:22
activity outreach from Russian
08:24
government high-level encouragement of
08:25
contacts through alternative channels
08:28
Gerald Demetrius transition era outreach
08:31
to incoming administration background
08:33
Carol

08:34

Demetrius *post-election* contact with the

08:37

incoming administration

08:38

Eric press and Tyrael the Meredith meat

08:41

is sensational

08:42

George later and Erik Prince arrange

08:46

Seychelles meeting with dimetric the

08:48

Seychelles meeting every princess living

08:50

with Steve man and after this Asian

08:52

strip Carrick Demetrius post-election

08:55

contact with Rick Gerson regarding

08:57

Russia

08:58

us-russia relations ambassador kiss lake

09:01

meeting with Jared Kushner and Michael

09:03

flame in Trump Towers following the

09:04

election general crush next meeting

09:06

would say gay go golf **Peter Evans**

09:10

outreach effort to the transition team

09:12

cat a page contact with Deputy Prime

09:15

Minister Arkady Duvall

09:18

contacts week and through Michael

09:21

t-phone United Nations vote on Israeli

09:24

settlements genetics sanctions against

09:27

Russia five prosecution and declination

09:31

decisions Russia actively show social

09:35

media campaign be Russian hacking and

09:38

dumping operations okay this is a page

09:41

175 within that one in section 1030

09:44

computer intrusion conspiracy you have a

09:47

broad grin and envy is this pretty much

09:51

redactors I saw him cause harm to

09:54

ongoing our manners but to is potential

09:58

1030 violation by a private person does

10:01

redacted Russian government our recent

10:03

contacts base 180 with indict Charlie

10:06

have a potential coordination conspiracy

10:10

and collusion to potential coordination

10:12

foreign agents statues FA RA and 18 USC

10:17

Section 951 government lures can be

10:23

found on page 181 application page 182

10:27

campaign finance overview of the

10:30

governing laws application to June 9th

10:34

12th meeting tower Dana value element

10:37

willfulness difficulty in value of

10:40

promise information application to

10:42

WikiLeaks

10:43

that's redacted questions over that's

10:46

also redacted willfulness constitutional

10:50

considerations page 190 analysis is

10:52

redacted false statement and obstruction

10:56

of investigation that's number four over

10:58

they will have an overview of governing

11:01

laws the application of certain

11:03

individuals and under be one-half george

11:06

papadapolis that's on 192 to is a

11:11

reductive of personal privacy three is

11:14

Michael flame for is **Michael Cohen** five

11:17

is connected

11:19

six is **Jeff Sessions** 7 is other

11:23

interviewed during the investigation

11:25

okay so this is page 5 of the again

11:28

we'll just talking about the table of

11:30

contents okay

11:31

the contents it's very interesting this

11:33

is going to be a sight coming it's very

11:35

interesting how this is all laid out and

11:37

how it was then applied to if whether

11:41
each one of those individuals actually
11:43
are we're who are basically uh the
11:46
briefs this statute right here potential
11:49
coordination foreign agents statutes FA
11:51
RA
11:52
and eighteen section *18 USC Section 951*
11:57
so it's interesting how they lay the
11:59
governing laws the application and also
12:01
whether there was any potential campaign
12:03
finance laws violations with this whole
12:06
thing
12:06
okay this matter so like again that's
12:08
all we we talked about the page right
12:10
now we're actually only a page 8 of this
12:14
448 page information so now let's get to
12:19
the meat and potatoes we just talked
12:20
about the actual introduction let's get
12:23
to the meat and potatoes okay so here we
12:25
go introduction to Volume one this
12:28
report is submitted to the Attorney
12:30
General
12:30
pursuant to 28 CFR section 608 C which

12:36
states that quote at the conclusion of
12:39
the special counsel's work he shall
12:42
provide the Attorney General or
12:44
confidential report explaining the
12:46
prosecution or declination decisions the
12:49
special counsel reached close quote
12:52
paragraph this Russian government
12:55
interfered in the 2016 presidential
12:58
election in sweeping and systematic
13:01
fashion evidence of Russian government's
13:04
operations began to surface in mid-2016
13:08
in June the Democratic National
13:11
Committee and in **cyber response team**
13:14
publicly announced that Russian hackers
13:18
had compromised its computer networks
13:22
releases of hacked material hacks that
13:26
public reporting soon and tributed it to
13:28
the Russian government began that same
13:31
month
13:32
additional releases followed in July
13:35
through the organization WikiLeaks with
13:38
further releases in October and Levin

13:42

in late July 2016 soon after WikiLeaks

13:46

first release of stolen documents of

13:49

foreign government contacted the FBI

13:52

about May 2016 encounter would trump

13:56

campaign foreign policy adviser George

14:00

papadopolis Papadopoulos has suggested

14:04

to a representative of that foreign

14:06

government that the Trump campaign had

14:09

received indications from Russia

14:11

government that it could assist the

14:14

campaign through the anonymous release

14:16

of information damaging Democratic

14:19

presidential candidate **Hillary Clinton**

14:21

that information from depth the FBI on

14:25

July 31st 2016 to open an investigation

14:29

into whether individuals with the Trump

14:33

campaign were coordinating with the

14:35

Russian government in its interference

14:38

activities that form two federal

14:43

agencies jointly announced that the

14:46

Russian government quote directed recent

14:49

compromises of emails from US persons

14:52

and institutions including US political

14:55

organizations close quote and quote

14:58

these thefts and disclosures are

15:02

intended to interfere with the u.s.

15:05

election process close quote

15:08

after the election in late December 2016

15:12

the United States imposed sanctions on

15:15

Russia for having interfered in the

15:18

election by early 2017 several

15:23

congressional committees were examining

15:26

Russia's interference in the election

15:29

within the executive branch these

15:32

investigatory efforts ultimately led to

15:34

the may 2017 appointment of special

15:38

counsel

15:39

Robert X Mueller the third the order

15:44

upon in the special counsel authorized

15:46

him to investigate quote the Russian

15:49

government's effort to interfere in the

15:51

2016 presidential elections close quote

15:54

include

15:55

any link or coordination between the

15:58
Russian government and individuals
16:00
associated with the Trump campaign as
16:03
set forth in detail in this report the
16:06
special counsels investigation
16:08
established that Russia interfered in
16:12
2016 presidential election principally
16:16
through two operations first Russian NAV
16:20
CANADA of social media campaign that
16:23
favored presidential candidate Donald J
16:26
Trump and disparaged presidential
16:29
candidate Hillary Clinton second of
16:33
Russian intelligence service conducted
16:37
computer intrusion operations against
16:40
enemies employees and volunteers on the
16:44
Clinton campaign and then release stolen
16:47
documents the investigation also
16:51
identified links between Russian
16:54
government and the Trump campaign so
16:57
what we're gonna do gonna start
16:58
highlight is something wanted to redact
17:00
but it can't redact anything so we're
17:02
gonna do some highlighting as we read

17:04

.okay

17:04

all right although the investigation

17:08

establish that government the Russian

17:10

government perceived it would benefit

17:12

from a trump administration or Trump

17:16

presidency and work to secure that

17:18

outcome they campaign I'm gonna start

17:22

this all over again although the

17:25

investigation established that the

17:27

Russian government perceived it would

17:30

benefit from a trump presidency and

17:33

worked to secure that outcome and that

17:35

the campaign expected it would benefit

17:39

electorally from information stolen and

17:42

release to the russian efforts the

17:45

investigation did not establish that

17:49

members of the Trump campaign conspired

17:51

or coordinated with the Russian

17:55

government in its election in different

17:58

activities so let me ask a question in

18:01

the sidebar so does that mean it's no

18:03

collusion no interference is it

18:07
basically Claire Trump and the campaign
18:09
folks well let's continue reading blog
18:13
we describe the evidentiary
18:15
considerations on dependent statements
18:18
about results of our investigation and
18:21
the special counsels decision and we
18:23
then provide an overview of the two
18:26
volumes of our report they report
18:29
describes actions and events that the
18:31
special counsel's office found to be
18:34
supported by evidence collected in our
18:37
investigation in some instances the
18:41
report points out the absence of
18:43
evidence or conflicts in the evidence
18:47
about a particular fact or event in
18:54
other instances when substantial
18:58
credible evidence enable the office to
19:01
reach a conclusion with confidence the
19:05
report states that the investigation
19:08
established that certain actions or
19:10
events occurred a statement that
19:19
investigation did not established

19:21
particular facts does not mean there was
19:25
no evidence this is very important a
19:27
statement that the investigation did not
19:30
establish particular facts does not mean
19:35
that there was no evidence of those
19:38
facts interesting in evaluating whether
19:44
evidence about corrective action of
19:46
multiple individuals constituted a crime
19:49
we applied the framework of conspiracy
19:53
law not the concept of collusion so when
19:58
when it was dealing with multiple
20:00
individuals framework conspicious
20:03
conspiracy law was applied not the
20:06
concept of collusion in so doing the
20:10
office recognized that the word collude
20:13
was used in communication with the
20:15
acting Attorney General confirming
20:17
certain aspects of the investigation
20:19
scope
20:20
that the term has frequently been
20:23
invoked in public reporting about the
20:26
investigation but collusion is not a

20:30
specific offense or theory of liability
20:35
found in the United States Code this go
20:38
ahead and highlight this real quick
20:40
but collusion is not a specific offense
20:44
or theory of liability found in the
20:48
United States code nor is it a term of
20:51
art in federal criminal law or this is
20:55
very important folks nor is it a term of
20:59
art in federal criminal prosecution so
21:03
I'm gonna pause real quick for quick
21:04
commentary so what does that really mean
21:06
if if the term collusion it's not a no
21:09
offense the reliability no is it a term
21:13
of art in federal criminal conspiracy
21:16
doesn't it if if you didn't look at it
21:19
from the word collusion and it's not a
21:21
crime does that doesn't mean that it
21:23
doesn't matter if if collusion didn't
21:26
happen well I don't know what do you
21:28
guys think just wait and leave a comment
21:30
on this middle section you can comment
21:32
at this audio book tell me what you

21:34

think also if you're the You Tube

21:35

channel go ahead and leave a comment

21:36

right there alright and let us know what

21:38

you think about this this particular

21:39

important spot on this stuff and that's

21:42

what we're coming up with this audio

21:43

book so we can kind of analyze exactly

21:45

what the thought process was in going

21:48

into this report okay let's continue for

21:52

those reasons the office focused on

21:56

analyzing questions of joint criminal

21:58

liability was on conspiracy as defined

22:02

in federal law in connection with that

22:06

analysis we addressed the factual

22:08

questions or the members of the Trump

22:11

campaign coordinated in terms that

22:14

appears in the appointment order with

22:17

Russian election interference activities

22:21

like collusion coordination does not

22:25

have a settled definition in criminal

22:28

law here we go again

22:29

like collusion coordination those

22:34
not have a settled definition in federal
22:37
criminal law we understood coordination
22:41
to require an agreement tak sit or
22:45
Express between with Trump campaign and
22:49
the Russian government on election in a
22:53
fairness that requires more than the two
22:56
parties taking action that were informed
22:59
or responsive to others action or
23:02
interests we apply the term coordination
23:05
in that sense when stating in the report
23:09
that investigation did not establish
23:12
that the Trump campaign coordinated with
23:17
the Russian government in his election
23:19
interference so that right there
23:23
explains it in this is page 10 of the
23:28
144 page documents okay
23:30
the report on an investigation consists
23:33
of two volumes again I can mention
23:34
previously this is volume 1 we're
23:36
talking about so here's what volume one
23:38
talks about volume one describes the
23:40
factual results of the special counsels

23:43
investigation of Russia's interference
23:46
in the 2016 presidential elections and
23:49
his interaction with a Trump campaign
23:53
okay second it describes the scope of
23:57
the investigation sections 2 & 3
24:00
describe the principal ways Russia
24:03
interfered in the 2016 presidential
24:06
election section 4 describes the links
24:08
between the Russian government and
24:10
individuals associated with the Trump
24:13
campaign section 5 sets forth the
24:16
special counsels charged in decisions
24:18
following - describes the president's
24:21
actions was the FBI's investigation into
24:24
Russians interference in the 2016
24:27
invested presidential election and
24:29
related matters and his actions towards
24:33
a special counselous investigations
24:35
falling to separately States its
24:38
framework and considerations that guided
24:41
the investigation
24:45
okay this is base three of the actual

24:50
document with the actual art but it's
24:53
page 11 of one now gonna page page 12
24:57
okay
24:58
executive summary - volume one again I'm
25:02
gonna tell you some of this stuff is for
25:03
adapted so we're just gonna keep reading
25:05
for guess to something less redacted
25:06
we're going to tell you redacted okay
25:09
Russia social media campaign the
25:12
internet research agency IRA carried out
25:16
the earliest Russian interference
25:19
operations identified by the
25:20
investigation social media campaign
25:23
designed to provoke and amplify
25:26
political and social discord in the
25:29
United States the IRA was based in st.
25:32
Petersburg Russia and received funding
25:35
from Russia all agog you forgive me
25:38
produce to him and companies he
25:43
controlled pretty good him is what a
25:46
little Prada to have ties to Russian
25:48
President Vladimir Putin the other parts

25:51

are redacted inmate 2014 the IRA sent

25:56

employees to the United States on an

25:59

intelligence gathering mission with

26:01

instructions on going meta redacted the

26:04

IR a little bit later use social media

26:07

accounts and interest groups will sow

26:09

discord in the United States political

26:12

system through what it terms information

26:14

warfare the campaign involved a

26:18

generalized program design in 2014 and

26:21

2015 to undermine the u.s. electoral

26:24

system there were targeted operations

26:27

that by early 2016

26:29

favored candidate Trump and disparage

26:33

candidate Clinton the IRS operation also

26:37

included the purchase of political

26:39

advertisements on social media in the

26:42

name of US persons enemies as well as

26:45

the staging of political rallies inside

26:48

the United States to organize rallies

26:51

IRA employees posed as US grass

26:54

rude enemies and persons and make

26:57
contact with Trump supporters and Trump
26:59
campaign officials in the United States
27:01
the investigation did not identify
27:03
evidence that any US persons conspired
27:05
or coordinated with the IRA section two
27:10
of this report details the offices
27:14
investigation of Russia's social media
27:16
campaign headline social Russian hacking
27:20
operations at the time that the IRA
27:23
operation began to focus on supporting
27:26
candidate Trump in early 2016 the
27:29
Russian government employed a second
27:31
form of interference cyber intrusions
27:34
also known as hacking and releases of
27:38
hacked materials damaging the Clinton
27:41
campaign the Russian intelligence
27:43
service known as the main intelligence
27:46
Directorate of the General Staff of the
27:48
Russian army also known as GRU carried
27:53
out these operations will repeat that
27:57
again I'm gonna highlight it right we
28:02
don't know what that means but the

28:04
Russian intelligence service known as
28:06
the main intelligence Directorate of the
28:09
General Staff of the Russian army
28:12
GRU carried out these operations in
28:17
March 2016 the GRU began hacking the
28:22
email accounts of Clinton campaign
28:24
volunteers and employees including
28:26
camping chairman John Podesta in April
28:31
2016 the GRU and hacked into the
28:34
computer networks of the Democratic
28:36
Congressional Campaign Committee DCCC
28:40
and the Democratic National Committee D
28:43
and C the GRU stole hundreds of
28:48
thousands of documents from the
28:51
compromised email accounts and networks
28:55
around the time that the DNC announced
28:58
in late June of 2016 Russian government
29:01
role and happiness networks the GRU
29:04
began disseminating stolen materials
29:07
through the fictitious online personas
29:10
coach DC licks ad gusoff or 2.0 GRE
29:16
later released additional materials to

29:18
organization WikiLeaks the presidential
29:24
campaign of Donald J Trump quote Trump
29:28
campaign or campaign showed interest in
29:30
WikiLeaks releases of documents and
29:33
welcomed their potential to damage
29:37
candidate Clinton beginning in June 2016
29:42
this is redacted due to the ongoing
29:45
manner forecast to the senior campaign
29:48
officials that WikiLeaks would release
29:51
information damaging to candidate
29:54
Clinton WikiLeaks first release came in
29:58
July 2016 around the same time candidate
30:02
Trump announced that he hoped Russia
30:06
would recover the email subscribers
30:08
missing from a private server used by
30:10
Clinton when she was Secretary of State
30:13
he later said that he was speaking
30:15
sarcastically when the highlight this
30:18
cuz this is on the news all the time
30:21
okay around the same time candidate
30:24
Trump announced that he hoped Russia
30:28
would recover emails describing a

30:32
missing described as missing from a
30:35
private server used by Clinton when she
30:37
was Secretary of State he later said
30:40
that he was speaking sarcastically the
30:43
rest of the sentence following data is
30:46
redacted to do to harm the ongoing

30:48
matter continuing WikiLeaks began
30:51
releasing Podesta stolen emails on
30:54
October 7 2016 less than an hour after
30:59
on US media outlet released video
31:02
considered damaging to candidate Trump
31:07
section 3 of this report details the
31:10
offices investigation into the Russian
31:13
hacker operation as well as other
31:17
efforts by Trump campaign supporters to
31:21
then Clinton related emails both headed
31:27
Russia contacts with the campaign the
31:32
social media campaign and the GRU
31:34
hacking Operation coincided with a
31:36
series of contacts between Trump
31:38
campaign officials and individuals with
31:40

ties to the Russian government the
31:42
office investigated whether those
31:43
contacts in fact they all resulted in
31:45
the campaign conspiring or coordinating
31:48
with Russia in his election interference
31:50
activities although the investigation
31:51
establish that the Russian government
31:52
who said it would benefit from a trump
31:54
presidency and work to secure that
31:56
outcome and that they can been expected
31:58
it would benefit electorate from the
32:00
information stolen and released through
32:01
Russia efforts the investigation did not
32:03
establish that members of the Trump
32:05
campaign conspired or coordinated with a
32:07
Russian government in its election
32:09
indifference activities the Russian
32:12
contacts consisted of business
32:14
connections offers of assistance to
32:16
campaign imitations for candidates Trump
32:18
and put in a meet in person invitations
32:20
for campaign officials and
32:21

representatives of the Russian
32:22
government in need and the policy
32:24
positions that can improve us-russian
32:26
relations section 4 of this report
32:30
details that contacts between Russia and
32:32
the Trump campaign during the campaign
32:34
and the transition periods the most
32:36
salient of which are summarized blog in
32:40
chronological order years 2015 some of
32:46
the earliest contacts were made in
32:47
connection with the Trump Organization
32:48
real estate projects in Russia known as
32:51
it from our Moscow Canada Trump signed a
32:54
letter of intent for Trump Tower Moscow
32:57
by November 2015 and in January 2016
33:01
trunk organization executive Michael
33:03
Cohen emailed and spoke about the
33:05
project with the office of Russian
33:07
government press secretary Dmitry Peskov
33:09
the Trump Organization pursued the
33:12
project to at least June 2016 including
33:15
by considering travel to Russia by : and
33:18

committed Trump
33:20
spring 2016 campaign foreign policy
33:25
adviser George papadopolis made early
33:28
contact with Joseph Masood a
33:31
london-based professor who had
33:32
connections to Russia
33:34
travelled to Moscow in April 2016
33:38
immediately upon his return from London
33:40
from that trip misfit told Papadopoulos
33:44
that the Russian government had caught
33:45
dirt on Hillary Clinton in the form of
33:48
thousands of emails going aboard and
33:51
highlight this request immediately upon
33:53
his return from that trip Massoud
33:56
Totalus and the Russian government had
33:59
dirt on Hillary Clinton him from of
34:02
thousands of emails thousands of emails
34:07
right one week later in the first week
34:11
of May 2016 Papadopoulos suggested to a
34:15
representative of a foreign government
34:17
that the Trump campaign had received
34:19
indications from the Russian government
34:20

that it could assist the campaign
34:23
through an anonymous release of
34:25
information damaging to Clinton
34:27
throughout that period of time for
34:30
several months thereafter
34:31
Papadopoulos worked with myths surd and
34:36
two Russian nationals to arrange a
34:38
meeting between campaign and the Russian
34:40
government no meeting took place summer
34:44
of 2016
34:46
Russia outreach to the Trump campaign
34:49
continued in the summer of 2016 as
34:51
candidate Trump was becoming the
34:54
presumptive Republican nominee for
34:56
president on June 9 2016 for example a
35:00
Russian lawyer met with senior Trump
35:03
campaign officials Donald Trump jr.
35:05
Jared Kushner and campaign Chairman Paul
35:08
Manafort to deliver what the email
35:10
proposing the media had described as
35:12
quote official documents and information
35:15
that would incriminate Hillary close
35:18

quote the materials were offered to
35:21
trump jr. as could part of Russia and
35:23
his government support for mr. Trump
35:26
close quote the written communication
35:28
setting up the meeting show that the
35:31
campaign anticipated receiving
35:32
information from Russia that could
35:34
assist kill it Trump's electoral
35:37
prospect but the Russian lawyer
35:39
presentation did not provide such
35:42
information days after June 9 meeting on
35:46
June 14 20s
35:48
in a cybersecurity firm and the DNC
35:50
announced that Rochelle government
35:53
hackers had infiltrated the DNC and
35:56
obtain access to opposition research on
35:59
Canada Trump among others
36:03
documents in July 2016 campaign foreign
36:08
policy advisor Carter page travelled in
36:11
his personal capacity to Moscow and gave
36:14
the keynote address at the New Economics
36:18
school Paige had lived and worked in
36:22

Russia between 2003 and 2007 after
36:26
returning to the United States Paige
36:28
became a clinic with at least two
36:30
Russian intelligence officers one of
36:33
whom was later charged in 2015 with
36:35
conspiracy to act as an unregistered
36:37
agent of Russia Paige's July 2 an
36:41
assistant trip to Moscow and his
36:43
advocacy for pro-russian foreign policy
36:46
drew media attention they campaigned and
36:49
distance itself from Paige and by late
36:52
September 2016 removed him from the
36:55
campaign July 2016 was also the month
37:01
WikiLeaks first released emails stolen
37:04
from the GRU from the DNC stolen by the
37:08
GRU from the DNC on July 22nd 2016
37:13
WikiLeaks posted thousands of internal
37:16
DNC documents revealing information
37:18
about the Clinton campaign within days
37:22
there was public reporting that US
37:25
intelligence agencies had quote high
37:28
confidence that the Russian government
37:30

was behind the theft of the emails and
37:32
the documents from the DNC and within
37:36
weeks of the release a foreign
37:37
government informed the FBI about its
37:41
May 2016 interaction with Papadopoulos
37:44
and his statement that the Russian
37:46
government could assist with Trump
37:48
campaign on July 31st 2016 based on the
37:52
foreign government reporting the FBI
37:54
opened an investigation
37:56
into potential coordination between the
37:59
Russian government and individuals
38:01
associated with the Trump campaign okay
38:03
we've seen this a lot coming up with the
38:05
news of late how the investigation
38:08
started so we're gonna go ahead and
38:09
highlight this within a week of the
38:12
release of foreign government inform the
38:15
FBI about its May 2016 interaction with
38:20
Papadopoulos and his statement that the
38:24
Russian government could assist the
38:27
Trump campaign on July 31st 2016 based
38:32

on the foreign governments reporting the
38:36
FB i-- opened an investigation into
38:40
potential coordination between the
38:43
russian government and individuals
38:46
associated with a trump campaign okay so
38:49
that's how this investigation started
38:51
you're gonna hear a lot of news about
38:53
how he got started in fact there might
38:55
be investigations about the
38:56
investigation so gonna continue reading
38:59
separately on August 2nd 2016 Trump
39:04
campaign chairman Paul Manafort met in
39:07
New York City with his longtime business
39:11
associate konstantin eliminate who the
39:17
FBI assesses to have ties to russian
39:20
intelligence okay
39:22
eliminate requested the meeting to
39:25
deliver in person a peace plan for
39:28
Ukraine the Manafort acknowledged to the
39:31
special Kansas office was a backdoor way
39:34
for Russia to control part of eastern
39:38
Ukraine both men believed the plan will
39:41

require candidate Trump's assent to
39:43
succeed where he to be elected president
39:47
they also discussed the status of the
39:51
campaign and the manifest strategy for
39:54
winning Democratic votes in Midwestern
39:57
states months before that meeting
40:00
Manafort had caused internal polling
40:05
data to be shared with kill me
40:08
and the sharing continued for some
40:11
peered after that time so months before
40:15
this meeting Manafort cost internal
40:19
polling data to be shared with clinic
40:22
for him official and the Sheraton
40:25
continued for some period after the
40:29
August meeting so I'm going to do a
40:31
little bit commentary right there so
40:33
does this make sense man while an effort
40:36
actually is in jail because he did
40:38
somebody's stuff even though the report
40:42
actually it's details and says for fact
40:44
that there was no coordination or
40:46
collusion that's a little bit confusing
40:50

okay let's continue fall of 2016 on
40:55

October 7 2016 the media released video
40:59

of candidate Trump speaking in graphic
41:02

terms about women years earlier which
41:05

was considered damaging to his
41:06

presidency less than an hour later
41:08

WikiLeaks made his second release
41:11

thousands of John Podesta email that had
41:14

been stolen by the GRU
41:15

in late March 2016 the FBI and other
41:19

government institutions where at the
41:21

time continuing their investigation of
41:23

suspected Russian government efforts to
41:26

interfere in the presidential elections
41:28

that same day October 7 the Department
41:31

of Homeland Security and the office of
41:33

Director of National Intelligence issued
41:36

a joint public statement that the
41:38

Russian government had directed recent
41:41

compromises of emails from US persons
41:43

and institutions including the u.s.
41:45

political organizations plus quote those
41:49

steps and the disclosures of the hacked
41:52
materials through the online platforms
41:55
such as WikiLeaks the statement
41:57
continued quote are intended to
41:59
interfere with the u.s. election process
42:02
close quote closed 2016 election
42:07
immediately after the November 8
42:10
election Russian government officials
42:11
impress prominent Russian businessmen
42:13
began trying to make inroads into the
42:15
new administration the most senior level
42:18
of the Russian government encouraged
42:20
these efforts the
42:21
should embassy make contact hours after
42:24
the election to congratulate
42:25
president-elect had to arrange a call
42:28
with President Putin several Russian
42:30
businessmen picked up the efforts from
42:33
their kirio Dmitry of the chief
42:37
executive officer of Russia's sovereign
42:39
wealth fund was among the Russians who
42:42
tried to make contact with the incoming
42:45

administration in early December of
42:47
business associates stared Dmitry - Erik
42:50
Prince a supporter of the Trump campaign
42:53
and an associate of senior Trump adviser
42:56
Steve Menon the midstream and translator
42:59
met face to face in January 2017 in the
43:03
socials and discuss us-russia relations
43:08
during the same period another business
43:11
associate introduced the midriff to a
43:13
friend of Jared Kushner who had not
43:15
served on the campaign on the transition
43:17
team Demetria and Kushner's friend
43:20
collaborated on a short written
43:22
reconciliation plan for the US and
43:24
Russia which Dimitrov implied had been
43:28
cleared to Putin the friend gave that
43:32
proposal to Kushner before the
43:34
inauguration and Kushner later gave
43:36
copies to Darren and incoming Secretary
43:38
of State Rex Tillerson pause continuing
43:49
on December 29 2016 then President Obama
43:56
imposed sanctions on Russia for having
43:59

NFL in the election incoming national
44:03
security advisor Michael Flynn called
44:04
Russia ambassador say gay kiss kiss lag
44:07
and a structured not to escalate the
44:10
situation in respond to the sanctions
44:12
the following day put Putin announced
44:15
that Russia would not take retaliatory
44:17
measures in response to the sanctions at
44:20
that time okay so that this may account
44:24
for why flint is going to prison because
44:27
it was an incoming national security
44:29
adviser and he called ambassador siggy
44:32
Kistler and
44:33
asked rusher not to escalate the
44:35
situation in response to the section was
44:38
he within his right to do that as an
44:41
incoming National Security Advisor even
44:44
though it was not officially a
44:46
transitionary period so that means that
44:49
may indicate why he's going to jail okay
44:51
before they put in then announced that
44:53
Russia would not take retaliatory
44:55

measures in response to the sanctions at
45:58
that time hours later president-elect
45:02
Trump tweeted great move on the delay by
45:06
putting close close the next day on
45:07
December 31st 2016
45:09
Kistler called flame and told him the
45:12
request had been received at the highest
45:14
levels and Russia had chosen not to
45:17
retaliate as a result of Flynn's request
45:19
this is very critical because this may
45:22
explain why flame because they said he
45:25
said something and he lied and and
45:27
that's why he is going to jail okay it
45:30
hasn't been sentenced yet I don't think
45:32
this is a brand new news in the if you
45:35
following this developments this is it
45:38
hasn't been sentenced but this is a key
45:40
part of why we think he's going to jail
45:43
end of commentary on July 6 2017 members
45:48
of the Intelligence Committee briefed
45:50
president-elect trunk on a joint
45:53
assessment drafted and coordinated among
45:57

the Central Intelligence Agency FBI and
46:00
the National Security Agency that
46:03
concluded with high confidence that
46:07
Russia had intervened in the election
46:09
through a variety of means to assist
46:12
Trump's candidacy and on Clinton's
46:16
Declassified version of the assessment
46:18
will publicly released that same day
46:21
between mid January 2017 and early
46:25
February 2017 three congressional
46:28
committees the house permanent Select
46:30
Committee on Intelligence hb-sgi the
46:34
Senate Select Committee on Intelligence
46:36
s SCR and the Senate Judicial Committee
46:39
s JC announced that they would conduct a
46:44
queries or had already begun conducted
46:47
Curry's into Russia interference in
46:49
election then FBI director James Comey
46:52
later confirmed the Congress the
46:55
existence of the FBI's investigation
46:57
into Russian interference and that had
47:00
begun before the election on March 20th
47:04

2017 in open session testimony before
47:08
the HP SC I call me stated I have been
47:13
authorized by the Department of Justice
47:15
to confirm that the FBI as part of our
47:19
counterintelligence mission is
47:21
investigated to Russia's government's
47:24
efforts to interfere in 2016
47:27
presidential election and that includes
47:30
investigating the nature of any links
47:31
between individuals associated with the
47:34
Trump campaign and the Russian
47:35
government and whether there was
47:37
coordination between the campaign and
47:39
Russian efforts and with any kind of
47:43
intelligence investigation this will
47:46
also include an assessment of whether
47:48
any crimes were committed can I
47:52
understand so the FBI was running a
47:55
counterintelligence investigation and
47:56
also looking into if there was any
47:58
crimes in the Comintern the
48:01
investigation continued on the dam
48:03

director Comey for the next several
48:05
weeks of the May 9th 2017 when President
48:08
Trump fired coming as FBI director an
48:13
action which is analyzed in volume 2 of
48:16
the report on May 17 2017 acting
48:22
Attorney General rod Rosenstein appoint
48:25
a special counsel and authorized him to
48:26
conduct the investigation that Comey had
48:29
confirmed in his congressional testimony
48:31
as well as matters arising directly from
48:34
the investigation and any other matters
48:38
which within the scope of 28 CFR
48:41
subsection 604 alpha which sonority
48:45
covers efforts to interfere with or
48:47
obstruct the investigation so the
48:50
appointment by their acting Attorney
48:54
General Rosen's then appointed a special
48:57
cancel that authorizing the consulate
48:59
investigation that commune had confirmed
49:01
in his congressional testimony as well
49:03
as matters arising from the
49:05
investigation and any other matters
49:07

within the scope of 28 CFR section 604 a
49:12
which generally covered efforts to
49:15
interfere or obstruct the investigation
49:19
so this is where this attorney general
49:20
this is commentary this were the
49:22
Attorney General's appointment then was
49:25
was was made public after Jeff's after
49:30
call me publicly disclosed the care
49:33
intelligence investigation then a
49:35
special counsel was then appointed if
49:38
you notice it was appointed to see if
49:42
there was matters within the scope of
49:44
the 28 CFR section 602 4a which also
49:50
includes a to see if there was
49:51
interference or obstruction so this is
49:54
where it becomes a little tricky okay
49:56
when why was the special counsel
49:58
appointed and what was their partner to
50:01
do and even after he was appointed they
50:04
did report conclusively or they did not
50:08
conclusively say if there was
50:10
interference or if there was obstruction
50:13

you be the judge go ahead and comment
50:16
blog if you're looking at this a little
50:18
bit YouTube or you listen to the
50:21
audiobook just go ahead and comment once
50:24
you get a chance okay and ever
50:25
commentary president Trump reacted
50:29
negatively to this special counsels
50:31
appointment he told advisors that it was
50:34
the end of his presidency sought to have
50:38
attorney general Jeff session all recuse
50:41
himself from the russia investigation
50:43
and to have the special counsel removed
50:45
and engaged in efforts to curtail the
50:48
special counsels investigation and
50:50
prevent the disclosure of evidence to it
50:53
including through public and private
50:55
contacts with potential witnesses those
50:57
that related actions are described and
51:00
analyzing following two of the reports
51:04
heading the special counsels charging
51:07
decisions in reaching the Charter
51:10
decisions described in volume one of the
51:11

report
51:12
the office determine whether the conduct
51:13
is found and knotted to a violation of
51:16
federal criminal law chargeable under
51:18
the principle of federal prosecution see
51:20
justice manual section 9 2 2700 each S
51:28
2018 the standard set forth in the
51:32
Justice Medal is whether the conduct
51:33
constitutes a crime if so whether
51:36
admissible evidence will probably be
51:38
sufficient of dinner sustain a
51:39
conviction and what are the process the
51:42
prosecution will serve a substantial
51:46
federal interest that could not be
51:48
adequately served by persecution
51:50
elsewhere or through non criminal
51:51
alternatives see justice manual section
51:55
nine through twenty seven dots two to
51:58
zero section five of the report provides
52:03
detailed explanation of the offices
52:06
chargin decisions which contain three
52:09
main components first the office
52:11

determined that Russia's two principal
52:14
interference operations in the 2016 US
52:17
presidential election though the social
52:20
media campaign and the hacking and
52:22
dumping of operations violated u.s.
52:25
criminal law the office determined I'm
52:29
going to say this again among uploaded
52:31
the office determined that Russia's two
52:34
principle interference operations in the
52:38
2016 US presidential election social
52:41
media campaign and the hacking and
52:44
dumping operations
52:45
violated US criminal law most of the
52:49
individuals and entities involved in the
52:51
social media campaign have been charged
52:53
with participated in the conspiracy to
52:56
defraud the United States back on the
52:59
money through deceptive acts the work of
53:02
federal agencies charged with regulating
53:05
foreign influence in u.s. elections as
53:08
well as related counts of identity theft
53:10
see United States vs Internet research
53:13

agency account number 18 - CR - 32 D DC
53:21

separately Russian intelligence officers
53:23

who carried out the hacking into the
53:26

Democratic Party computers and the
53:29

personal email accounts of individuals
53:31

affiliated with the Clinton campaign
53:33

conspire to violate among other federal
53:36

laws the federal computer intrusion
53:39

statute and they have been charged C
53:43

United States persons ethics to a camera
53:48

number 18 C R - 2 1 v DD C the rest of
53:55

this source is actually redacted this is
53:57

haunted ongoing matter and personal
53:59

privacy second while the investigation
54:03

identified numerous links between
54:05

individuals with ties to the Russian
54:07

government and individuals associated
54:09

with the Trump campaign the evidence was
54:13

not sufficient to support criminal
54:15

charges among those things the evidence
54:19

was not sufficient to charge any
54:21

campaign official as an unregistered
54:24

agent of the Russian government or other
54:27
Russian principle and our evidence about
54:30
the June 9 2016 meeting and the
54:33
WikiLeaks releases of hacked material
54:36
was not sufficient to charge a criminal
54:39
campaign finance violation
54:42
further the evidence was not sufficient
54:45
to charge that any member of the Trump
54:47
campaign conspired with representatives
54:50
of the Russian government to interfere
54:52
in the 2016 election so when you hear
54:58
President Trump and some Republicans
55:00
this is the commentary saying no
55:03
collusion no you know no interference
55:06
and you know it's a clean bill this is
55:09
probably why where they get that
55:11
information from okay and I'm gonna read
55:13
that again so we're more clear further
55:15
the evidence was not sufficient to
55:18
charge that any member of the Trump
55:20
campaign conspired with representatives
55:23
of the Russian government to interfere
55:25

in the 2016
55:28
election but let me ask you guys this
55:30
it's listen closely if this was Obama
55:34
what do you think would happen if this
55:39
happened under Obama what would it
55:41
happen in fact last week you know
55:45
special adviser to then President Obama
55:48
Valerie Jarrett made a statement and I
55:52
quote he said if this was Obama Obama
55:53
would have been locked up in a
55:55
nanosecond in a nanosecond this was
55:58
Obama so what do you guys think
56:00
go ahead and comment blog the YouTube
56:02
video if you think Obama would have been
56:03
locked up if this involved him and his
56:06
folks what do you think is this a double
56:09
standard I don't know comment blog and
56:11
let me know what you guys think okay in
56:12
a commenter I'm gonna go ahead and
56:14
continue third the investigation
56:17
established that several individuals
56:19
affiliated with the Trump campaign lie
56:22

to the office and to Congress about the
56:25
interactions with the Russian affiliated
56:27
individuals and related matters those
56:30
lies materially impaired investigation
56:32
of the Russian election interference the
56:35
office charged some of those lies as
56:37
violations of federal false statement
56:39
statutes former national security
56:41
adviser Michael Flynn pleaded guilty to
56:44
lying about his interactions with
56:45
Russian ambassador his Lea act during
56:49
the transition period George papadopolis
56:51
of foreign policy advisor during the
56:53
campaign period pleaded guilty to lying
56:56
to investigators about inter alia the
56:59
nature and timing of his interaction
57:02
with Joseph missus the professor who
57:05
taught Papadopoulos that the Russian had
57:08
dirt all candidate Clinton in a form of
57:11
thousands of emails from a trump
57:15
organization attorney Michael Cohen
57:17
pleaded guilty to making false
57:19

statements to Congress about the Moscow
57:22
project the rest of that statement is
57:24
redacted and in February 2019 the US
57:29
District Court for the District of
57:30
Columbia found that Manafort lied to the
57:33
office and the grand jury concerning his
57:36
interaction and communication with
57:39
Konstantin Kalama neck about Trump
57:42
campaign polling data and a peace plan
57:45
for Ukraine the office investigated
57:49
several other events that had been
57:52
publicly reported to include potential
57:55
Russian related contacts okay for
57:58
example the investigation establish that
58:00
interaction between Russia
58:02
ambassador Kistler and the Trump
58:04
campaign officials both at the
58:07
candidates April 2016 foreign policy
58:09
speech in Washington DC and during the
58:12
week of the Republican National
58:13
Convention where brief public and non
58:17
subs substances and the investigation
58:20

did not establish that one campaign
58:23
official effort to delete a portion of
58:27
the Republican Party's platform on
58:29
providing assistance to Ukraine where
58:32
are the taken at the behest of candidate
58:35
Trump or Russia the investigation also
58:38
did not establish that a meeting between
58:40
case lag and sessions in September 2016
58:42
as sessions Senate office included any
58:46
more than a passing mention of the
58:48
presidential campaign the investigation
58:51
did not always yield admissible
58:53
information or testimony or a complete
58:56
picture of the activities undertaken by
58:59
subject of the investigation some
59:02
investigation invoked the Fifth
59:04
Amendment right against compelled
59:06
self-incrimination and were not in the
59:09
offices judgment appropriate candidates
59:11
for grants of immunity the office
59:15
limited its pursuit of other witnesses
59:18
and information such as information no
59:20

to attorneys or individuals claiming to
59:21
be members of the media in light of the
59:23
internal Department of Justice policies
59:26
see example justice manual subsection 9
59:30
that - 13.4 hundred comma
59:35
13.4 ten some of the information
59:38
obtained via court process moreover was
59:41
presumptively covered by legal privilege
59:45
and was screened from investigators by
59:48
filter
59:49
or teat team even when individuals
59:53
testified or agreed to be interviewed
59:55
they sometimes provided information that
59:57
was false or incomplete leading to some
60:01
of the false statement charges described
60:03
above and the office faced practical
60:07
limits on his ability to assess relevant
60:10
evidence as well numerous witnesses and
60:14
subjects lie lived abroad and documents
60:18
were held as at the United States
60:20
further the office learned that some of
60:24
the individuals were edited or whose
60:26

conducts were investigated including
60:28
some associated with the Trump campaign
60:30
deleted relevant communication or
60:34
communicated during the relevant period
60:36
using applications that featured
60:38
encryption or that do not provide for
60:41
long term retention of data or
60:44
communication records in such cases the
60:46
office was not able to collaborate
60:49
witness statements to comparison to
60:52
contemporaneous communications or fully
60:55
question witnesses about statements that
60:57
appeared inconsistent with other known
61:00
facts accordingly while this report
61:04
embodies factual and legal
61:06
determinations that the office believes
61:08
to be accurate and complete to the
61:10
greatest extent possible
61:12
even these identify gaps the office
61:15
cannot rule out the possibility that the
61:18
unavailable information would shed
61:20
additional light on or cast in a new
61:25

light it invents this crap in the report
61:27
so in other words there might be
61:29
information out there that nobody has
61:30
again this is a commentary it might be
61:33
information out there that they did not
61:35
have available to them and consequently
61:38
they don't know for a fact if that
61:40
information could shed new light or cast
61:43
a new light on on the events okay so
61:46
that's very important so there might be
61:48
stuff like that I would not know about
61:49
the end of commentary new section the
61:53
special counsel's investigation on May
61:58
7th
62:00
20:17 Deputy Attorney General rod Jay
62:03
Rosen stand then serving as acting
62:06
Attorney General for the Russia
62:08
investigation following the refusal of
62:11
former attorney general Jeff Sessions on
62:13
March 2 2016 appointed the special
62:17
counsel quote to investigate Russian
62:21
interference with the 2016 presidential
62:24

elections and related matters
62:26
close quote highlight that on March 2nd
62:30
2016 appointed special counsel to
62:33
investigate Russian interference with
62:38
the 2016 presidential elections and
62:40
related matters office of Deputy
62:45
Attorney General Order number three nine
62:49
15.2 zero one seven appointment of
62:52
special counsel to investigate Russian
62:55
interference with the 2016 presidential
62:57
election and related matters May 17 27
63:01
teen appointment orders relying on quote
63:05
the authority vested close quote in the
63:08
acting Attorney General including 28 USC
63:13
subsection 509 510 and 515 the active
63:19
Attorney General ordered the appointment
63:23
of a special counsel quote in order to
63:26
discharge the acting Attorney General's
63:29
responsibility to provide supervision
63:31
and management of the Department of
63:33
Justice and to ensure a full and
63:35
thorough investigation of the Russian
63:37

government's effort to interfere in the
63:39
2016 presidential election most World
63:43
Order introduction the special cancel
63:47
the order stated what is authorized to
63:51
conduct the investigation confirmed by
63:54
then FBI director james b Comey in
63:59
testimony before the house permanent
64:01
Select Committee on Intelligence on
64:03
march 22 2017 including one any leaks
64:11
and all coordination between the Russian
64:13
government and individuals associated
64:14
with the campaign of President Donald
64:17
Trump and - and it matters that arose or
64:20
may arise directly from the
64:22
investigation and three any man other
64:26
matters within the scope of 28 CFR
64:30
section 604 a appointment orders B
64:35
session 600 dots for of course the
64:38
special counsel the authority to
64:40
investigate and prosecute federal crimes
64:44
committed in the course of and we intend
64:47
to interfere with the special counsels
64:50

investigation sergeants perjury

64:52

obstruction of justice

64:53

destruction evidence and intimidation of

64:56

witnesses 28 CFR section $600 for a the

65:02

authority to investigate any matters

65:04

that arose directly from the

65:06

investigation permit orders a Bravo to

65:10

cover similar crimes that may have

65:12

prepared during the course of the FBI

65:14

confirmed investigation before special

65:17

counsels equipment if the special counsel

65:20

believed it is necessary and appropriate

65:23

the order further provided quote the

65:26

special counsel is authorized and

65:28

prosecuted federal crimes arising from

65:31

the investigation of these matters and

65:35

finally the acting Attorney General made

65:37

applicable section 600 of 4 to 600 the

65:43

10 of title 28 of the federal of the

65:47

Code of Federal Regulations all right so

65:51

basically to sum all this up it says if

65:53

you can do some investigation and

65:56

basically prosecute pops they were lying
66:00
or cutting stuff up okay
66:02
that's the addition from that's how come
66:04
some people are going to jail for life
66:07
in the country brick
66:18
we'll return from the great we're gonna
66:20
do right now we're gonna stop and we're
66:23
gonna continue reading this at a later
66:24
time okay so yeah just just be on the
66:27
lookout and uh go ahead and comment if
66:30
you haven't already commented on some of
66:31
the stuff that we talked about yes a
66:33
chance to grant do this comments okay
66:35
and what we're gonna do is gonna
66:36
continue reading this and we want to
66:38
come back and the next time you see this
66:42
you're gonna have a full accounting of
66:43
move already done okay
English (auto-generated)
English (auto-generated)
Show chat replay
07:56
Orlick there is a strike consulting work
07:59
political consulting work cost Anakin
08:01
eliminate contacts with power mana first

08:04
time with the Trump campaign Paul
08:06
Manafort joins the campaign for
08:07
manifests campaign period context for
08:09
mana first to campaign period were
08:12
meeting with Kostas still a chemical
08:14
emanation United States post resignation
08:17
activities post election a transition
08:19
period contacts immediate post-election
08:22
activity outreach from Russian
08:24
government high-level encouragement of
08:25
contacts through alternative channels
08:28
Gerald Demetrius transition era outreach
08:31
to incoming administration background
08:33
Carol
08:34
Demetrius post-election contact with the
08:37
incoming administration
08:38
Eric press and Tyrael the Meredith meat
08:41
is sensational
08:42
George later and Erik Prince arrange
08:46
Seychelles meeting with dimetric the
08:48
Seychelles meeting every princess living
08:50
with Steve man and after this Asian

08:52
strip Carrick Demetrius post-election
08:55
contact with Rick Gerson regarding
08:57
Russia
08:58
us-russia relations ambassador kiss lake
09:01
meeting with Jared Kushner and Michael
09:03
flame in Trump Towers following the
09:04
election general crush next meeting
09:06
would say gay go golf Peter Evans
09:10
outreach effort to the transition team
09:12
cat a page contact with Deputy Prime
09:15
Minister Arkady Duvall
09:18
contacts week and through Michael
09:21
t-phone United Nations vote on Israeli
09:24
settlements genetics sanctions against
09:27
Russia five prosecution and declination
09:31
decisions Russia actively show social
09:35
media campaign be Russian hacking and
09:38
dumping operations okay this is a page
09:41
175 within that one in section 1030
09:44
computer intrusion conspiracy you have a
09:47
broad grin and envy is this pretty much
09:51
redactors I saw him cause harm to

09:54

ongoing our manners but to is potential

09:58

1030 violation by a private person does

10:01

redacted Russian government our recent

10:03

contacts base 180 with indict Charlie

10:06

have a potential coordination conspiracy

10:10

and collusion to potential coordination

10:12

foreign agents statues FA RA and 18 USC

10:17

Section 951 government lures can be

10:23

found on page 181 application page 182

10:27

campaign finance overview of the

10:30

governing laws application to June 9th

10:34

12th meeting tower Dana value element

10:37

willfulness difficulty in value of

10:40

promise information application to

10:42

WikiLeaks

10:43

that's redacted questions over that's

10:46

also redacted willfulness constitutional

10:50

considerations page 190 analysis is

10:52

redacted false statement and obstruction

10:56

of investigation that's number four over

10:58

they will have a overview of governing

11:01

laws the application of certain

11:03
individuals and under be one-half george
11:06
papadapolis that's on 192 to is a
11:11
reductive of personal privacy three is
11:14
michael flame for is michael cohen five
11:17
is connected
11:19
six is jeff sessions 7 is other
11:23
interviewed during the investigation
11:25
okay so this is page 5 of the again
11:28
we'll just talking about the table of
11:30
contents okay
11:31
the contents it's very interesting this
11:33
is going to be a sight coming it's very
11:35
interesting how this is all laid out and
11:37
how it was then applied to if whether
11:41
each one of those individuals actually
11:43
are we're who are basically uh the
11:46
briefs this statute right here potential
11:49
coordination foreign agents statutes FA
11:51
RA
11:52
and eighteen section 18 USC Section 951
11:57
so it's interesting how they lay the
11:59
governing laws the application and also

12:01

whether there was any potential campaign

12:03

finance laws violations with this whole

12:06

thing

12:06

okay this matter so like again that's

12:08

all we we talked about the page right

12:10

now we're actually only a page 8 of this

12:14

448 page information so now let's get to

12:19

the meat and potatoes we just talked

12:20

about the actual introduction let's get

12:23

to the meat and potatoes okay so here we

12:25

go introduction to Volume one this

12:28

report is submitted to the Attorney

12:30

General

12:30

pursuant to 28 CFR section 608 C which

12:36

states that quote at the conclusion of

12:39

the special counsels work he shall

12:42

provide the Attorney General or

12:44

confidential report explaining the

12:46

prosecution or declination decisions the

12:49

special counsel reached close quote

12:52

paragraph this Russian government

12:55

interfered in the 2016 presidential

12:58
election in sweeping and systematic
13:01
fashion evidence of Russian government's
13:04
operations began to surface in mid-2016
13:08
in June the Democratic National
13:11
Committee and in cyber response team
13:14
publicly announced that Russian hackers
13:18
had compromised its computer networks
13:22
releases of hacked material hacks that
13:26
public reporting soon and tributed it to
13:28
the Russian government began that same
13:31
month
13:32
additional releases followed in July
13:35
through the organization WikiLeaks with
13:38
further releases in October and Levin
13:42
in late July 2016 soon after WikiLeaks
13:46
first release of stolen documents of
13:49
foreign government contacted the FBI
13:52
about May 2016 encounter would trump
13:56
campaign foreign policy adviser George
14:00
papadopolis Papadopoulos has suggested
14:04
to a representative of that foreign
14:06
government that the Trump campaign had

14:09
received indications from Russia
14:11
government that it could assist the
14:14
campaign through the anonymous release
14:16
of information damaging Democratic
14:19
presidential candidate Hillary Clinton
14:21
that information from depth the FBI on
14:25
July 31st 2016 to open an investigation
14:29
into whether individuals with the Trump
14:33
campaign were coordinating with the
14:35
Russian government in its interference
14:38
activities that form two federal
14:43
agencies jointly announced that the
14:46
Russian government quote directed recent
14:49
compromises of emails from US persons
14:52
and institutions including US political
14:55
organizations close quote and quote
14:58
these thefts and disclosures are
15:02
intended to interfere with the u.s.
15:05
election process close quote
15:08
after the election in late December 2016
15:12
the United States imposed sanctions on
15:15
Russia for having interfered in the

15:18

election by early 2017 several

15:23

congressional committees were examining

15:26

Russia's interference in the election

15:29

within the executive branch these

15:32

investigatory efforts ultimately led to

15:34

the may 2017 appointment of special

15:38

counsel

15:39

Robert X Mueller the third the order

15:44

upon in the special counsel authorized

15:46

him to investigate quote the Russian

15:49

government's effort to interfere in the

15:51

2016 presidential elections close quote

15:54

include

15:55

any link or coordination between the

15:58

Russian government and individuals

16:00

associated with the Trump campaign as

16:03

set forth in detail in this report the

16:06

special counsels investigation

16:08

established that Russia interfered in

16:12

2016 presidential election principally

16:16

through two operations first Russian NAV

16:20

CANADA of social media campaign that

16:23
favored presidential candidate Donald J
16:26
Trump and disparaged presidential
16:29
candidate Hillary Clinton second of
16:33
Russian intelligence service conducted
16:37
computer intrusion operations against
16:40
enemies employees and volunteers on the
16:44
Clinton campaign and then release stolen
16:47
documents the investigation also
16:51
identified links between Russian
16:54
government and the Trump campaign so
16:57
what we're gonna do gonna start
16:58
highlight is something wanted to redact
17:00
but it can't redact anything so we're
17:02
gonna do some highlighting as we read
17:04
okay
17:04
all right although the investigation
17:08
establish that government the Russian
17:10
government perceived it would benefit
17:12
from a trump administration or Trump
17:16
presidency and work to secure that
17:18
outcome they campaign I'm gonna start
17:22
this all over again although the

17:25
investigation established that the
17:27
Russian government perceived it would
17:30
benefit from a trump presidency and
17:33
worked to secure that outcome and that
17:35
the campaign expected it would benefit
17:39
electorally from information stolen and
17:42
release to the russian efforts the
17:45
investigation did not establish that
17:49
members of the Trump campaign conspired
17:51
or coordinated with the Russian
17:55
government in its election in different
17:58
activities so let me ask a question in
18:01
the sidebar so does that mean it's no
18:03
collusion no interference is it
18:07
basically Claire Trump and the campaign
18:09
folks well let's continue reading blog
18:13
we describe the evidentiary
18:15
considerations on dependent statements
18:18
about results of our investigation and
18:21
the special counsels decision and we
18:23
then provide an overview of the two
18:26
volumes of our report they report

18:29
describes actions and events that the
18:31
special counsel's office found to be
18:34
supported by evidence collected in our
18:37
investigation in some instances the
18:41
report points out the absence of
18:43
evidence or conflicts in the evidence
18:47
about a particular fact or event in
18:54
other instances when substantial
18:58
credible evidence enable the office to
19:01
reach a conclusion with confidence the
19:05
report states that the investigation
19:08
established that certain actions or
19:10
events occurred a statement that
19:19
investigation did not established
19:21
particular facts does not mean there was
19:25
no evidence this is very important a
19:27
statement that the investigation did not
19:30
establish particular facts does not mean
19:35
that there was no evidence of those
19:38
facts interesting in evaluating whether
19:44
evidence about corrective action of
19:46
multiple individuals constituted a crime

19:49
we applied the framework of conspiracy
19:53
law not the concept of collusion so when
19:58
when it was dealing with multiple
20:00
individuals framework conspicious
20:03
conspiracy law was applied not the
20:06
concept of collusion in so doing the
20:10
office recognized that the word collude
20:13
was used in communication with the
20:15
acting Attorney General confirming
20:17
certain aspects of the investigation
20:19
scope
20:20
that the term has frequently been
20:23
invoked in public reporting about the
20:26
investigation but collusion is not a
20:30
specific offense or theory of liability
20:35
found in the United States Code this go
20:38
ahead and highlight this real quick
20:40
but collusion is not a specific offense
20:44
or theory of liability found in the
20:48
United States code nor is it a term of
20:51
art in federal criminal law or this is
20:55
very important folks nor is it a term of

20:59
art in federal criminal prosecution so
21:03
I'm gonna pause real quick for quick
21:04
commentary so what does that really mean
21:06
if if the term collusion it's not a no
21:09
offense the reliability no is it a term
21:13
of art in federal criminal conspiracy
21:16
doesn't it if if you didn't look at it
21:19
from the word collusion and it's not a
21:21
crime does that doesn't mean that it
21:23
doesn't matter if if collusion didn't
21:26
happen well I don't know what do you
21:28
guys think just wait and leave a comment
21:30
on this middle section you can comment
21:32
at this audio book tell me what you
21:34
think also if you're the You Tube
21:35
channel go ahead and leave a comment
21:36
right there alright and let us know what
21:38
you think about this this particular
21:39
important spot on this stuff and that's
21:42
what we're coming up with this audio
21:43
book so we can kind of analyze exactly
21:45
what the thought process was in going

21:48

into this report okay let's continue for

21:52

those reasons the office focused on

21:56

analyzing questions of joint criminal

21:58

liability was on conspiracy as defined

22:02

in federal law in connection with that

22:06

analysis we addressed the factual

22:08

questions or the members of the Trump

22:11

campaign coordinated in terms that

22:14

appears in the appointment order with

22:17

Russian election interference activities

22:21

like collusion coordination does not

22:25

have a settled definition in criminal

22:28

law here we go again

22:29

like collusion coordination those

22:34

not have a settled definition in federal

22:37

criminal law we understood coordination

22:41

to require an agreement tak sit or

22:45

Express between with Trump campaign and

22:49

the Russian government on election in a

22:53

fairness that requires more than the two

22:56

parties taking action that were informed

22:59

or responsive to others action or

23:02
interests we apply the term coordination
23:05
in that sense when stating in the report
23:09
that investigation did not establish
23:12
that the Trump campaign coordinated with
23:17
the Russian government in his election
23:19
interference so that right there
23:23
explains it in this is page 10 of the
23:28
144 page documents okay
23:30
the report on an investigation consists
23:33
of two volumes again I can mention
23:34
previously this is volume 1 we're
23:36
talking about so here's what volume one
23:38
talks about volume one describes the
23:40
factual results of the special counsels
23:43
investigation of Russia's interference
23:46
in the 2016 presidential elections and
23:49
his interaction with a Trump campaign
23:53
okay second it describes the scope of
23:57
the investigation sections 2 & 3
24:00
describe the principal ways Russia
24:03
interfered in the 2016 presidential
24:06
election section 4 describes the links

24:08
between the Russian government and
24:10
individuals associated with the Trump
24:13
campaign section 5 sets forth the
24:16
special counsels charged in decisions
24:18
following - describes the president's
24:21
actions was the FBI's investigation into
24:24
Russians interference in the 2016
24:27
invested presidential election and
24:29
related matters and his actions towards
24:33
a special counselous investigations
24:35
falling to separately States its
24:38
framework and considerations that guided
24:41
the investigation
24:45
okay this is base three of the actual
24:50
document with the actual art but it's
24:53
page 11 of one now gonna page page 12
24:57
okay
24:58
executive summary - volume one again I'm
25:02
gonna tell you some of this stuff is for
25:03
adapted so we're just gonna keep reading
25:05
for guess to something less redacted
25:06
we're going to tell you redacted okay

25:09
Russia social media campaign the
25:12
internet research agency IRA carried out
25:16
the earliest Russian interference
25:19
operations identified by the
25:20
investigation social media campaign
25:23
designed to provoke and amplify
25:26
political and social discord in the
25:29
United States the IRA was based in st.
25:32
Petersburg Russia and received funding
25:35
from Russia all agog you forgive me
25:38
produce to him and companies he
25:43
controlled pretty good him is what a
25:46
little Prada to have ties to Russian
25:48
President Vladimir Putin the other parts
25:51
are redacted inmate 2014 the IRA sent
25:56
employees to the United States on an
25:59
intelligence gathering mission with
26:01
instructions on going meta redacted the
26:04
IR a little bit later use social media
26:07
accounts and interest groups will sow
26:09
discord in the United States political
26:12
system through what it terms information

26:14

warfare the campaign involved a

26:18

generalized program design in 2014 and

26:21

2015 to undermine the u.s. electoral

26:24

system there were targeted operations

26:27

that by early 2016

26:29

favored candidate Trump and disparage

26:33

candidate Clinton the IRS operation also

26:37

included the purchase of political

26:39

advertisements on social media in the

26:42

name of US persons enemies as well as

26:45

the staging of political rallies inside

26:48

the United States to organize rallies

26:51

IRA employees posed as US grass

26:54

rude enemies and persons and make

26:57

contact with Trump supporters and Trump

26:59

campaign officials in the United States

27:01

the investigation did not identify

27:03

evidence that any US persons conspired

27:05

or coordinated with the IRA section two

27:10

of this report details the offices

27:14

investigation of Russia's social media

27:16

campaign headline social Russian hacking

27:20
operations at the time that the IRA
27:23
operation began to focus on supporting
27:26
candidate Trump in early 2016 the
27:29
Russian government employed a second
27:31
form of interference cyber intrusions
27:34
also known as hacking and releases of
27:38
hacked materials damaging the Clinton
27:41
campaign the Russian intelligence
27:43
service known as the main intelligence
27:46
Directorate of the General Staff of the
27:48
Russian army also known as GRU carried
27:53
out these operations will repeat that
27:57
again I'm gonna highlight it right we
28:02
don't know what that means but the
28:04
Russian intelligence service known as
28:06
the main intelligence Directorate of the
28:09
General Staff of the Russian army
28:12
GRU carried out these operations in
28:17
March 2016 the GRU began hacking the
28:22
email accounts of Clinton campaign
28:24
volunteers and employees including
28:26
camping chairman John Podesta in April

28:31
2016 the GRU and hacked into the
28:34
computer networks of the Democratic
28:36
Congressional Campaign Committee DCCC
28:40
and the Democratic National Committee D
28:43
and C the GRU stole hundreds of
28:48
thousands of documents from the
28:51
compromised email accounts and networks
28:55
around the time that the DNC announced
28:58
in late June of 2016 Russian government
29:01
role and happiness networks the GRU
29:04
began disseminating stolen materials
29:07
through the fictitious online personas
29:10
coach DC licks ad gusoff or 2.0 GRE
29:16
later released additional materials to
29:18
organization WikiLeaks the presidential
29:24
campaign of Donald J Trump quote Trump
29:28
campaign or campaign showed interest in
29:30
WikiLeaks releases of documents and
29:33
welcomed their potential to damage
29:37
candidate Clinton beginning in June 2016
29:42
this is redacted due to the ongoing
29:45
manner forecast to the senior campaign

29:48
officials that WikiLeaks would release
29:51
information damaging to candidate
29:54
Clinton WikiLeaks first release came in
29:58
July 2016 around the same time candidate
30:02
Trump announced that he hoped Russia
30:06
would recover the email subscribers
30:08
missing from a private server used by
30:10
Clinton when she was Secretary of State
30:13
he later said that he was speaking
30:15
sarcastically when the highlight this
30:18
cuz this is on the news all the time
30:21
okay around the same time candidate
30:24
Trump announced that he hoped Russia
30:28
would recover emails describing a
30:32
missing described as missing from a
30:35
private server used by Clinton when she
30:37
was Secretary of State he later said
30:40
that he was speaking sarcastically the
30:43
rest of the sentence following data is
30:46
redacted to do to harm the ongoing
30:48
matter continuing WikiLeaks began
30:51
releasing Podesta stolen emails on

30:54

October 7 2016 less than an hour after

30:59

on US media outlet released video

31:02

considered damaging to candidate Trump

31:07

section 3 of this report details the

31:10

offices investigation into the Russian

31:13

hacker operation as well as other

31:17

efforts by Trump campaign supporters to

31:21

then Clinton related emails both headed

31:27

Russia contacts with the campaign the

31:32

social media campaign and the GRU

31:34

hacking Operation coincided with a

31:36

series of contacts between Trump

31:38

campaign officials and individuals with

31:40

ties to the Russian government the

31:42

office investigated whether those

31:43

contacts in fact they all resulted in

31:45

the campaign conspiring or coordinating

31:48

with Russia in his election interference

31:50

activities although the investigation

31:51

establish that the Russian government

31:52

who said it would benefit from a trump

31:54

presidency and work to secure that

31:56
outcome and that they can been expected
31:58
it would benefit electorate from the
32:00
information stolen and released through
32:01
Russia efforts the investigation did not
32:03
establish that members of the Trump
32:05
campaign conspired or coordinated with a
32:07
Russian government in its election
32:09
indifference activities the Russian
32:12
contacts consisted of business
32:14
connections offers of assistance to
32:16
campaign imitations for candidates Trump
32:18
and put in a meet in person invitations
32:20
for campaign officials and
32:21
representatives of the Russian
32:22
government in need and the policy
32:24
positions that can improve us-russian
32:26
relations section 4 of this report
32:30
details that contacts between Russia and
32:32
the Trump campaign during the campaign
32:34
and the transition periods the most
32:36
salient of which are summarized blog in
32:40
chronological order years 2015 some of

32:46
the earliest contacts were made in
32:47
connection with the Trump Organization
32:48
real estate projects in Russia known as
32:51
it from our Moscow Canada Trump signed a
32:54
letter of intent for Trump Tower Moscow
32:57
by November 2015 and in January 2016
33:01
trunk organization executive Michael
33:03
Cohen emailed and spoke about the
33:05
project with the office of Russian
33:07
government press secretary Dmitry Peskov
33:09
the Trump Organization pursued the
33:12
project to at least June 2016 including
33:15
by considering travel to Russia by : and
33:18
committed Trump
33:20
spring 2016 campaign foreign policy
33:25
adviser George papadopolis made early
33:28
contact with Joseph Masood a
33:31
london-based professor who had
33:32
connections to Russia
33:34
travelled to Moscow in April 2016
33:38
immediately upon his return from London
33:40
from that trip misfit told Papadopoulos

33:44

that the Russian government had caught

33:45

dirt on Hillary Clinton in the form of

33:48

thousands of emails going aboard and

33:51

highlight this request immediately upon

33:53

his return from that trip Massoud

33:56

Totalus and the Russian government had

33:59

dirt on Hillary Clinton him from of

34:02

thousands of emails thousands of emails

34:07

right one week later in the first week

34:11

of May 2016 Papadopoulos suggested to a

34:15

representative of a foreign government

34:17

that the Trump campaign had received

34:19

indications from the Russian government

34:20

that it could assist the campaign

34:23

through an anonymous release of

34:25

information damaging to Clinton

34:27

throughout that period of time for

34:30

several months thereafter

34:31

Papadopoulos worked with myths surd and

34:36

two Russian nationals to arrange a

34:38

meeting between campaign and the Russian

34:40

government no meeting took place summer

34:44
of 2016
34:46
Russia outreach to the Trump campaign
34:49
continued in the summer of 2016 as
34:51
candidate Trump was becoming the
34:54
presumptive Republican nominee for
34:56
president on June 9 2016 for example a
35:00
Russian lawyer met with senior Trump
35:03
campaign officials Donald Trump jr.
35:05
Jared Kushner and campaign Chairman Paul
35:08
Manafort to deliver what the email
35:10
proposing the media had described as
35:12
quote official documents and information
35:15
that would incriminate Hillary close
35:18
quote the materials were offered to
35:21
trump jr. as could part of Russia and
35:23
his government support for mr. Trump
35:26
close quote the written communication
35:28
setting up the meeting show that the
35:31
campaign anticipated receiving
35:32
information from Russia that could
35:34
assist kill it Trump's electoral
35:37
prospect but the Russian lawyer

35:39
presentation did not provide such
35:42
information days after June 9 meeting on
35:46
June 14 20s
35:48
in a cybersecurity firm and the DNC
35:50
announced that Rochelle government
35:53
hackers had infiltrated the DNC and
35:56
obtain access to opposition research on
35:59
Canada Trump among others
36:03
documents in July 2016 campaign foreign
36:08
policy advisor Carter page travelled in
36:11
his personal capacity to Moscow and gave
36:14
the keynote address at the New Economics
36:18
school Paige had lived and worked in
36:22
Russia between 2003 and 2007 after
36:26
returning to the United States Paige
36:28
became a clinic with at least two
36:30
Russian intelligence officers one of
36:33
whom was later charged in 2015 with
36:35
conspiracy to act as an unregistered
36:37
agent of Russia Paige's July 2 an
36:41
assistant trip to Moscow and his
36:43
advocacy for pro-russian foreign policy

36:46
drew media attention they campaigned and
36:49
distance itself from Paige and by late
36:52
September 2016 removed him from the
36:55
campaign July 2016 was also the month
37:01
WikiLeaks first released emails stolen
37:04
from the GRU from the DNC stolen by the
37:08
GRU from the DNC on July 22nd 2016
37:13
WikiLeaks posted thousands of internal
37:16
DNC documents revealing information
37:18
about the Clinton campaign within days
37:22
there was public reporting that US
37:25
intelligence agencies had quote high
37:28
confidence that the Russian government
37:30
was behind the theft of the emails and
37:32
the documents from the DNC and within
37:36
weeks of the release a foreign
37:37
government informed the FBI about its
37:41
May 2016 interaction with Papadopoulos
37:44
and his statement that the Russian
37:46
government could assist with Trump
37:48
campaign on July 31st 2016 based on the
37:52
foreign government reporting the FBI

37:54
opened an investigation
37:56
into potential coordination between the
37:59
Russian government and individuals
38:01
associated with the Trump campaign okay
38:03
we've seen this a lot coming up with the
38:05
news of late how the investigation
38:08
started so we're gonna go ahead and
38:09
highlight this within a week of the
38:12
release of foreign government inform the
38:15
FBI about its May 2016 interaction with
38:20
Papadopoulos and his statement that the
38:24
Russian government could assist the
38:27
Trump campaign on July 31st 2016 based
38:32
on the foreign governments reporting the
38:36
FB i-- opened an investigation into
38:40
potential coordination between the
38:43
russian government and individuals
38:46
associated with a trump campaign okay so
38:49
that's how this investigation started
38:51
you're gonna hear a lot of news about
38:53
how he got started in fact there might
38:55
be investigations about the

38:56

investigation so gonna continue reading

38:59

separately on August 2nd 2016 Trump

39:04

campaign chairman Paul Manafort met in

39:07

New York City with his longtime business

39:11

associate konstantin eliminate who the

39:17

FBI assesses to have ties to russian

39:20

intelligence okay

39:22

eliminate requested the meeting to

39:25

deliver in person a peace plan for

39:28

Ukraine the Manafort acknowledged to the

39:31

special Kansas office was a backdoor way

39:34

for Russia to control part of eastern

39:38

Ukraine both men believed the plan will

39:41

require candidate Trump's assent to

39:43

succeed where he to be elected president

39:47

they also discussed the status of the

39:51

campaign and the manifest strategy for

39:54

winning Democratic votes in Midwestern

39:57

states months before that meeting

40:00

Manafort had caused internal polling

40:05

data to be shared with kill me

40:08

and the sharing continued for some

40:11

peered after that time so months before

40:15

this meeting Manafort cost internal

40:19

polling data to be shared with clinic

40:22

for him official and the Sheraton

40:25

continued for some period after the

40:29

August meeting so I'm going to do a

40:31

little bit commentary right there so

40:33

does this make sense man while an effort

40:36

actually is in jail because he did

40:38

somebody's stuff even though the report

40:42

actually it's details and says for fact

40:44

that there was no coordination or

40:46

collusion that's a little bit confusing

40:50

okay let's continue fall of 2016 on

40:55

October 7 2016 the media released video

40:59

of candidate Trump speaking in graphic

41:02

terms about women years earlier which

41:05

was considered damaging to his

41:06

presidency less than an hour later

41:08

WikiLeaks made his second release

41:11

thousands of John Podesta email that had

41:14

been stolen by the GRU

41:15
in late March 2016 the FBI and other
41:19
government institutions where at the
41:21
time continuing their investigation of
41:23
suspected Russian government efforts to
41:26
interfere in the presidential elections
41:28
that same day October 7 the Department
41:31
of Homeland Security and the office of
41:33
Director of National Intelligence issued
41:36
a joint public statement that the
41:38
Russian government had directed recent
41:41
compromises of emails from US persons
41:43
and institutions including the u.s.
41:45
political organizations plus quote those
41:49
steps and the disclosures of the hacked
41:52
materials through the online platforms
41:55
such as WikiLeaks the statement
41:57
continued quote are intended to
41:59
interfere with the u.s. election process
42:02
close quote closed 2016 election
42:07
immediately after the November 8
42:10
election Russian government officials
42:11
impress prominent Russian businessmen

42:13
began trying to make inroads into the
42:15
new administration the most senior level
42:18
of the Russian government encouraged
42:20
these efforts the
42:21
should embassy make contact hours after
42:24
the election to congratulate
42:25
president-elect had to arrange a call
42:28
with President Putin several Russian
42:30
businessmen picked up the efforts from
42:33
their kirio Dmitry of the chief
42:37
executive officer of Russia's sovereign
42:39
wealth fund was among the Russians who
42:42
tried to make contact with the incoming
42:45
administration in early December of
42:47
business associates stared Dmitry - Erik
42:50
Prince a supporter of the Trump campaign
42:53
and an associate of senior Trump adviser
42:56
Steve Menon the midstream and translator
42:59
met face to face in January 2017 in the
43:03
socials and discuss us-russia relations
43:08
during the same period another business
43:11
associate introduced the midriff to a

43:13
friend of Jared Kushner who had not
43:15
served on the campaign on the transition
43:17
team Demetria and Kushner's friend
43:20
collaborated on a short written
43:22
reconciliation plan for the US and
43:24
Russia which Dimitrov implied had been
43:28
cleared to Putin the friend gave that
43:32
proposal to Kushner before the
43:34
inauguration and Kushner later gave
43:36
copies to Darren and incoming Secretary
43:38
of State Rex Tillerson pause continuing
43:49
on December 29 2016 then President Obama
43:56
imposed sanctions on Russia for having
43:59
NFL in the election incoming national
44:03
security advisor Michael Flynn called
44:04
Russia ambassador say gay kiss kiss lag
44:07
and a structured not to escalate the
44:10
situation in respond to the sanctions
44:12
the following day put Putin announced
44:15
that Russia would not take retaliatory
44:17
measures in response to the sanctions at
44:20
that time okay so that this may account

44:24

for why flint is going to prison because

44:27

it was an incoming national security

44:29

adviser and he called ambassador siggy

44:32

Kistler and

44:33

asked rusher not to escalate the

44:35

situation in response to the section was

44:38

he within his right to do that as an

44:41

incoming National Security Advisor even

44:44

though it was not officially a

44:46

transitionary period so that means that

44:49

may indicate why he's going to jail okay

44:51

before they put in then announced that

44:53

Russia would not take retaliatory

44:55

measures in response to the sanctions at

44:58

that time hours later president-elect

45:02

Trump tweeted great move on the delay by

45:06

putting close close the next day on

45:07

December 31st 2016

45:09

Kistler called flame and told him the

45:12

request had been received at the highest

45:14

levels and Russia had chosen not to

45:17

retaliate as a result of Flynn's request

45:19
this is very critical because this may
45:22
explain why flame because they said he
45:25
said something and he lied and and
45:27
that's why he is going to jail okay it
45:30
hasn't been sentenced yet I don't think
45:32
this is a brand new news in the if you
45:35
following this developments this is it
45:38
hasn't been sentenced but this is a key
45:40
part of why we think he's going to jail
45:43
end of commentary on July 6 2017 members
45:48
of the Intelligence Committee briefed
45:50
president-elect trunk on a joint
45:53
assessment drafted and coordinated among
45:57
the Central Intelligence Agency FBI and
46:00
the National Security Agency that
46:03
concluded with high confidence that
46:07
Russia had intervened in the election
46:09
through a variety of means to assist
46:12
Trump's candidacy and on Clinton's
46:16
Declassified version of the assessment
46:18
will publicly released that same day
46:21
between mid January 2017 and early

46:25
February 2017 three congressional
46:28
committees the house permanent Select
46:30
Committee on Intelligence hb-sgi the
46:34
Senate Select Committee on Intelligence
46:36
s SCR and the Senate Judicial Committee
46:39
s JC announced that they would conduct a
46:44
queries or had already begun conducted
46:47
Curry's into Russia interference in
46:49
election then FBI director James Comey
46:52
later confirmed the Congress the
46:55
existence of the FBI's investigation
46:57
into Russian interference and that had
47:00
begun before the election on March 20th
47:04
2017 in open session testimony before
47:08
the HP SC I call me stated I have been
47:13
authorized by the Department of Justice
47:15
to confirm that the FBI as part of our
47:19
counterintelligence mission is
47:21
investigated to Russia's government's
47:24
efforts to interfere in 2016
47:27
presidential election and that includes
47:30
investigating the nature of any links

47:31
between individuals associated with the
47:34
Trump campaign and the Russian
47:35
government and whether there was
47:37
coordination between the campaign and
47:39
Russian efforts and with any kind of
47:43
intelligence investigation this will
47:46
also include an assessment of whether
47:48
any crimes were committed can I
47:52
understand so the FBI was running a
47:55
counterintelligence investigation and
47:56
also looking into if there was any
47:58
crimes in the Comintern the
48:01
investigation continued on the dam
48:03
director Comey for the next several
48:05
weeks of the May 9th 2017 when President
48:08
Trump fired coming as FBI director an
48:13
action which is analyzed in volume 2 of
48:16
the report on May 17 2017 acting
48:22
Attorney General rod Rosenstein appoint
48:25
a special counsel and authorized him to
48:26
conduct the investigation that Comey had
48:29
confirmed in his congressional testimony

48:31
as well as matters arising directly from
48:34
the investigation and any other matters
48:38
which within the scope of 28 CFR
48:41
subsection 604 alpha which sonority
48:45
covers efforts to interfere with or
48:47
obstruct the investigation so the
48:50
appointment by their acting Attorney
48:54
General Rosen's then appointed a special
48:57
cancel that authorizing the consulate
48:59
investigation that commune had confirmed
49:01
in his congressional testimony as well
49:03
as matters arising from the
49:05
investigation and any other matters
49:07
within the scope of 28 CFR section 604 a
49:12
which generally covered efforts to
49:15
interfere or obstruct the investigation
49:19
so this is where this attorney general
49:20
this is commentary this were the
49:22
Attorney General's appointment then was
49:25
was was made public after Jeff's after
49:30
call me publicly disclosed the care
49:33
intelligence investigation then a

49:35
special counsel was then appointed if
49:38
you notice it was appointed to see if
49:42
there was matters within the scope of
49:44
the 28 CFR section 602 4a which also
49:50
includes a to see if there was
49:51
interference or obstruction so this is
49:54
where it becomes a little tricky okay
49:56
when why was the special counsel
49:58
appointed and what was their partner to
50:01
do and even after he was appointed they
50:04
did report conclusively or they did not
50:08
conclusively say if there was
50:10
interference or if there was obstruction
50:13
you be the judge go ahead and comment
50:16
blog if you're looking at this a little
50:18
bit YouTube or you listen to the
50:21
audiobook just go ahead and comment once
50:24
you get a chance okay and ever
50:25
commentary president Trump reacted
50:29
negatively to this special counsels
50:31
appointment he told advisors that it was
50:34
the end of his presidency sought to have

50:38
Attorney General Jeff Sessions all recuse
50:41
himself from the russia investigation
50:43
and to have the special counsel removed
50:45
and engaged in efforts to curtail the
50:48
special counsel's investigation and
50:50
prevent the disclosure of evidence to it
50:53
including through public and private
50:55
contacts with potential witnesses those
50:57
that related actions are described and
51:00
analyzing following two of the reports
51:04
heading the special counsels charging
51:07
decisions in reaching the Charter
51:10
decisions described in volume one of the
51:11
report
51:12
the office determine whether the conduct
51:13
is found and knotted to a violation of
51:16
federal criminal law chargeable under
51:18
the principle of federal prosecution see
51:20
justice manual section 9 2 2700 each S
51:28
2018 the standard set forth in the
51:32
Justice Medal is whether the conduct
51:33
constitutes a crime if so whether

51:36
admissible evidence will probably be
51:38
s
sufficient to sustain a
51:39
conviction and *what are the process of the*
51:42
prosecution will serve a substantial
51:46
federal interest that could not be
51:48
adequately served by prosecution
51:50
elsewhere or through non criminal
51:51
alternatives see justice manual section
51:55
nine through twenty seven dots two to
51:58
zero section five of the report provides
52:03
detailed explanation of the office's
52:06
charging decisions which contain three
52:09
main components first the office
52:11
determined that Russia's two principal
52:14
interference operations in the 2016 US
52:17
presidential election though the social
52:20
media campaign and the hacking and
52:22
dumping of operations violated u.s.
52:25
criminal law the office determined I'm
52:29
going to say this again among uploaded
52:31
the office determined that Russia's two
52:34

principle interference operations in the
52:38
2016 US presidential election social
52:41
media campaign and the hacking and
52:44
dumping operations
52:45
violated US criminal law most of the
52:49
individuals and entities involved in the
52:51
social media campaign have been charged
52:53
with participated in the conspiracy to
52:56
defraud the United States back on the
52:59
money through deceptive acts the work of
53:02
federal agencies charged with regulating
53:05
foreign influence in u.s. elections as
53:08
well as related counts of identity theft
53:10
see United States vs Internet research
53:13
agency account number 18 - CFR - 32 D DC
53:21
separately Russian intelligence officers
53:23
who carried out the hacking into the
53:26
Democratic Party computers and the
53:29
personal email accounts of individuals
53:31
affiliated with the Clinton campaign
53:33
conspire to violate among other federal
53:36
laws the federal computer intrusion
53:39

statute and they have been charged C
53:43

United States persons ethics to a camera
53:48

number 18 CFR - 2 1 v DD C the rest of
53:55

this source is actually redacted this is
53:57

haunted ongoing matter and personal
53:59

privacy second while the investigation
54:03

identified numerous links between
54:05

individuals with ties to the Russian
54:07

government and *individuals associated*
54:09

with the Trump campaign the evidence was
54:13

not sufficient to support criminal
54:15

charges among those things the evidence
54:19

was not sufficient to charge any
54:21

campaign official as an unregistered
54:24

agent of the Russian government or other
54:27

Russian principle and our evidence about
54:30

the June 9 2016 meeting and the
54:33

WikiLeaks releases of hacked material
54:36

was not sufficient to charge a criminal
54:39

campaign finance violation
54:42

further the evidence was not sufficient
54:45

to charge that any member of the Trump
54:47

campaign conspired with representatives
54:50
of the Russian government to interfere
54:52
in the 2016 election so when you hear
54:58
President Trump and some Republicans
55:00
this is the commentary saying no
55:03
collusion no you know the inference
55:06
and you know it's a clean bill this is
55:09
probably why where they get that
55:11
information from okay and I'm gonna read
55:13
that again so we're more clear further
55:15
the evidence was not sufficient to
55:18
charge that any member of the Trump
55:20
campaign conspired with representatives
55:23
of the Russian government to interfere
55:25
in the 2016
55:28
election but let me ask you guys this
55:30
it's listen closely *if this was **Obama***
55:34
what do you think would happen if this
55:39
happened under Obama what would it
55:41
happen in fact last week you know
55:45
special adviser to then President Obama
55:48
Valerie Jarrett made a statement and I
55:52

quote he said if this was Obama, Obama
55:53
would have been locked up in a
55:55
nanosecond in a nanosecond this was
55:58
Obama so what do you guys think
56:00
of the analysis and how no charges resulted in the impeachment?
56:02
Comment on the blog if you think Obama would have been
56:03
locked up if this involved him and his
56:06
folks what do you think? Is this a double
56:09
standard? I don't know, comment on blog and
56:11
let me know what you guys think okay in
56:12
a commenter I'm gonna go ahead and
56:14
continue third the investigation
56:17
established that several individuals
56:19
affiliated with the Trump campaign lie
56:22
to the office and to Congress about the
56:25
interactions with the Russian affiliated
56:27
individuals and related matters those
56:30
lies materially impaired investigation
56:32
of the Russian election interference the
56:35
office charged some of those lies as
56:37
violations of federal false statement
56:39
statutes former national security
56:41

adviser Michael Flynn pleaded guilty to
56:44
lying about his interactions with
56:45
Russian ambassador his Lea act during
56:49
the transition period **George Papadopolis**
56:51
of foreign policy advisor during the
56:53
campaign period pleaded guilty to lying
56:56
to investigators about inter alia the
56:59
nature and timing of his interaction
57:02
with Joseph missus the professor who
57:05
taught **Papadopoulos** that the Russian had
57:08
dirt all candidate Clinton in a form of
57:11
thousands of emails from a trump
57:15
organization attorney Michael Cohen
57:17
pleaded guilty to making false
57:19
statements to Congress about the Moscow
57:22
project the rest of that statement is
57:24
redacted and in February 2019 the US
57:29
District Court for the District of
57:30
Columbia found that Manafort lied to the
57:33
office and the grand jury concerning his
57:36
interaction and communication with
57:39
Konstantin Kalama neck about Trump
57:42

campaign polling data and a peace plan

57:45

for Ukraine the office investigated

57:49

several other events that had been

57:52

publicly reported to include potential

57:55

Russian related contacts okay for

57:58

example the investigation establish that

58:00

interaction between Russia

58:02

ambassador Kistler and the Trump

58:04

campaign officials both at the

58:07

candidates April 2016 foreign policy

58:09

speech in Washington DC and during the

58:12

week of the Republican National

58:13

Convention where brief public and non

58:17

subs substances and the investigation

58:20

did not establish that one campaign

58:23

official effort to **delete a portion of**

58:27

the Republican Party's platform on

58:29

providing assistance to Ukraine were

58:32

taken at the behest of candidate

58:35

Trump or Russia the investigation also

58:38

did not establish that a meeting between

58:40

case lag and sessions in September 2016

58:42
as sessions Senate office included any
58:46
more than a passing mention of the
58:48
presidential campaign the investigation
58:51
did not always yield admissible
58:53
information or testimony or a complete
58:56
picture of the activities undertaken by
58:59
subject of the investigation some
59:02
investigation invoked the Fifth
59:04
Amendment right against compelled
59:06
self-incrimination and were not in the
59:09
offices judgment appropriate candidates
59:11
for grants of immunity the office
59:15
limited its pursuit of other witnesses
59:18
and information such as information no
59:20
to attorneys or individuals claiming to
59:21
be members of the media in light of the
59:23
internal Department of Justice policies
59:26
see example justice manual subsection 9
59:30
that - 13.4 hundred comma
59:35
13.4 ten some of the information
59:38
obtained via court process moreover was
59:41
presumptively covered by legal privilege

59:45
and was screened from investigators by
59:48
filter
59:49
or teat team even when individuals
59:53
testified or agreed to be interviewed
59:55
they sometimes provided information that
59:57
was false or incomplete leading to some
60:01
of the false statement charges described
60:03
above and the office faced practical
60:07
limits on his ability to assess relevant
60:10
evidence as well numerous witnesses and
60:14
subjects lie lived abroad and documents
60:18
were held as at the United States
60:20
further the office learned that some of
60:24
the individuals were edited or whose
60:26
conducts were investigated including
60:28
some associated with the Trump campaign
60:30
deleted relevant communication or
60:34
communicated during the relevant period
60:36
using applications that featured
60:38
encryption or that do not provide for
60:41
long term retention of data or
60:44
communication records in such cases the

60:46
office was not able to collaborate
60:49
witness statements to comparison to
60:52
contemporaneous communications or fully
60:55
question witnesses about statements that
60:57
appeared inconsistent with other known
61:00
facts accordingly while this report
61:04
embodies factual and legal
61:06
determinations that the office believes
61:08
to be accurate and complete to the
61:10
greatest extent possible
61:12
even these identify gaps the office
61:15
cannot rule out the possibility that the
61:18
unavailable information would shed
61:20
additional light on or cast in a new
61:25
light it invents this crap in the report
61:27
so in other words there might be
61:29
information out there that nobody has
61:30
again this is a commentary it might be
61:33
information out there that they did not
61:35
have available to them and consequently
61:38
they don't know for a fact if that
61:40
information could shed new light or cast

61:43
a new light on on the events okay so
61:46
that's very important so there might be
61:48
stuff like that I would not know about
61:49
the end of commentary new section the
61:53
special counsel's investigation on May
61:58
7th
62:00
20:17 Deputy Attorney General Rod Jay
62:03
Rosen stand then serving as acting
62:06
Attorney General for the Russian
62:08
investigation following the refusal of
62:11
former attorney general Jeff Sessions on
62:13
March 2 2016 appointed the special
62:17
counsel quote to investigate Russian
62:21
interference with the 2016 presidential
62:24
elections and related matters
62:26
close quote highlight that on March 2nd
62:30
2016 appointed special counsel to
62:33
investigate Russian interference with
62:38
the 2016 presidential elections and
62:40
related matters office of Deputy
62:45
Attorney General Order number three nine
62:49
15.2 zero one seven appointment of

62:52
special counsel to investigate Russian
62:55
interference with the 2016 presidential
62:57
election and related matters May 17 2017
63:01
teen appointment orders relying on quote
63:05
the authority vested close quote in the
63:08
acting Attorney General including *28 USC*
63:13
subsection 509 510 and 515 the active
63:19
Attorney General ordered the appointment
63:23
of a special counsel quote in order to
63:26
discharge the acting Attorney General's
63:29
responsibility to provide supervision
63:31
and management of the Department of
63:33
Justice and to ensure a full and
63:35
thorough investigation of the Russian
63:37
government's effort to interfere in the
63:39
2016 presidential election most World
63:43
Order introduction the special cancel
63:47
the order stated what is authorized to
63:51
conduct the investigation confirmed by
63:54
*then FBI Director **James B. Comey** in*
63:59
testimony before the house permanent
64:01
Select Committee on Intelligence on

64:03

march 22 2017 including one any leaks

64:11

and all coordination between the Russian

64:13

government and individuals associated

64:14

with the campaign of President Donald

64:17

Trump and - and it matters that arose or

64:20

may arise directly from the

64:22

investigation and three any man other

64:26

matters within the scope of 28 CFR

64:30

section 604 an appointment orders B

64:35

session 600 dots for of course the

64:38

special counsel the authority to

64:40

investigate and prosecute federal crimes

64:44

committed in the course of and we intend

64:47

to interfere with the special counsels

64:50

investigation sergeants perjury

64:52

obstruction of justice

64:53

destruction evidence and intimidation of

64:56

witnesses 28 CFR section 600 for a the

65:02

authority to investigate any matters

65:04

that arose directly from the

65:06

investigation permit orders a Bravo to

65:10

cover similar crimes that may have

65:12
prepared during the course of the FBI
65:14
confirmed investigation before special
65:17
counsels equipment if the special counsel
65:20
believed it is necessary and appropriate
65:23
the order further provided quote the
65:26
special counsel is authorized and
65:28
prosecuted federal crimes arising from
65:31
the investigation of these matters and
65:35
finally the acting Attorney General made
65:37
applicable section 600 of 4 to 600 the
65:43
10 of title 28 of the federal of the
65:47
Code of Federal Regulations all right so
65:51
basically to sum all this up it says if
65:53
you can do some investigation and
65:56
basically prosecute pops they were lying
66:00
or cutting stuff up okay
66:02
that's the addition from that's how come
66:04
some people are going to jail for life
66:07
in the country brick
66:18
we'll return from the great we're gonna
66:20
do right now we're gonna stop and we're
66:23
gonna continue the analysis this at a matter

66:24

time okay so yeah just just be on the

66:27

lookout and uh go ahead and comment if

66:30

you haven't already commented on some of

66:31

the stuff that we talked about yes a

66:33

chance to grant do this comments okay

66:35

and what we're gonna do is gonna

66:36

continue the analysis and we want to

66:38

come back and the next time you see this

66:42

you're gonna have a full accounting of

66:43